HOW THE MOON CAME TO BE

A CHINESE LEGEND

retold by Jan M. Mike
illustrated by Andrea Arroyo

Scott Foresman

Editorial Offices: Glenview, Illinois • New York, New York
Sales Offices: Reading, Massachusetts • Duluth, Georgia
Glenview, Illinois • Carrollton, Texas • Menlo Park, California

Long ago, there was no moon. There were no stars sparkling in the night sky.

One evening, a poor boy named Ya La hurried home to his sister, Ni Wo. He had lost track of time peddling his carved wooden toys in the city. The day sun had set.

Close to home, Ya La heard rustling in the bushes. He began to run. But he had only gone a few steps before he tripped and fell.

"Oh, how I wish the night sky weren't so dark," Ya La shouted.

The words had barely left his mouth when a bright light filled the sky. A new, hot night sun blazed above him. Ya La ran home to his sister. But he did not find her in the sleeping quarters. The night sun had awakened her.

Many days and nights passed. The day sun continued to shine. The new night sun continued to shine too. No one could sleep in the hot, bright light. In the fields, the plants turned brown. People grew thin and tired. They were angry and unhappy. They had little food and no sleep. No one would buy the clever toys Ya La was peddling in the city.

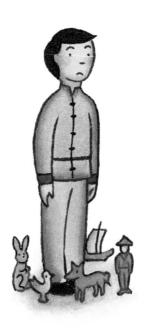

"Was it your wish that made this night sun?"
Ni Wo asked her brother one night.

"I don't know," Ya La said. "I have tried to
wish it away. But it will not go."

"We must do more than wish," Ni Wo said.
"We must go to the wise man in the mountain.
He will know what to do."

The journey was long and hard. At first roads led them past rich houses with ponds and servants' quarters. Then they left the city and walked along smaller paths through brown forests and dry grasslands. For many warm days and many hot nights Ya La and Ni Wo trudged on. Finally they reached the wise man's cave.

"I know why you are here," the wise man said. "Ya La, you are a good archer. You must shoot this night sun out of the sky. And you, Ni Wo, are a great weaver. You must help your brother. You are bound together by blood."

"But I cannot shoot an arrow that high," Ya La said.

"An archer is only as good as his tools. Here is what you must do," the wise man said.

Ya La and Ni Wo listened to the man for a long time. They learned what they must do. First Ni Wo cut off her long hair and began to weave it into a net. She worked for many days. She made sure the net was strong.

Then they left the wise man and began to climb the mountain. Higher and higher they climbed. Finally they reached the den of a fierce tiger. Ya La and Ni Wo spread the net of hair over the mouth of the tiger's den.

The tiger leaped from her den. She became tangled in the net. She roared and clawed. But Ni Wo's net was strong. Ya La reached out and plucked one long hair from the tiger's tail. Then Ni Wo whisked the net away. The tiger ran off unharmed.

Tucking the tiger's hair away, Ya La and his sister continued on their journey. They climbed over the mountain and down the other side. They went on until they reached a large forest. They tied Ni Wo's net between the two tallest trees.

A huge deer leaped between the trees, catching his antlers in the net. He twisted and turned. But Ni Wo's net was strong. Ya La reached out and took a piece of the deer's antler. Then Ni Wo pulled the net away. The deer ran off unharmed.

Ya La and Ni Wo bound together the tiger hair and the deer antler. Then they took them to the wise man. With his help, they used the animals' gifts to make a bow and three sharp arrows. Then brother and sister left once more. In the middle of the hot night they climbed to the top of the mountain.

Ya La stood on the mountaintop. He looked up into the bright night sky. Ya La took a deep breath. He pulled his tiger bowstring back as far as it would go. Into the sky his arrow flew. Up, up, it raced into the center of the blazing night sun.

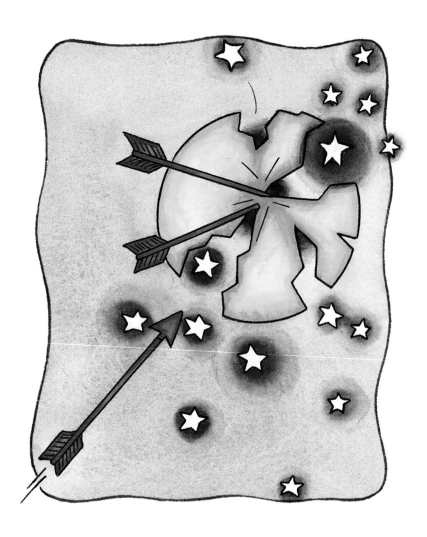

He shot his second arrow. It sped through the air and hit the heart of the night sun. Ya La shot off his third and final arrow. When the last arrow struck the night sun, a bright light filled the sky.

Ya La and Ni Wo fell to the ground. They covered their eyes. A huge rumbling filled the night air. Then the rumbling stopped and the light was gone.

Ni Wo and Ya La looked up at the sky. Tiny stars twinkled across the black sky. Cool moonlight flooded the mountaintop. The blazing night sun was gone.

The brother and sister returned home. Their friends greeted them with great joy.

From that day on, the night sky was dark. But it wasn't too dark. And so it remains to this very day. If you look out your bedroom window at night, you can see the sparkling stars and the cool, white moon.

They are gifts from Ni Wo and Ya La.